Are We An "Us"?

Also by Jerry Scott and Jim Borgman

Zits: Sketchbook 1
Growth Spurt: Zits Sketchbook 2
Don't Roll Your Eyes at Me, Young Man!: Zits Sketchbook 3

Humongous Zits: A Zits Treasury

Are We An "Us"?

A Zits® Collection
Sketchbook #4

by JERRY SCOTT and JIM BORGMAN

Andrews McMeel
Publishing

Kansas City

For Martin Garhart,
who flipped the light switch on.
—J.B.

To Ernie Bushmiller.
I owe you one, man.
—J.S.

8

9

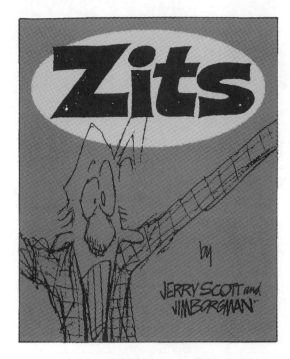

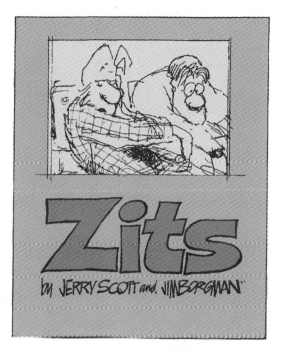

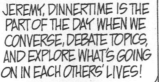

19

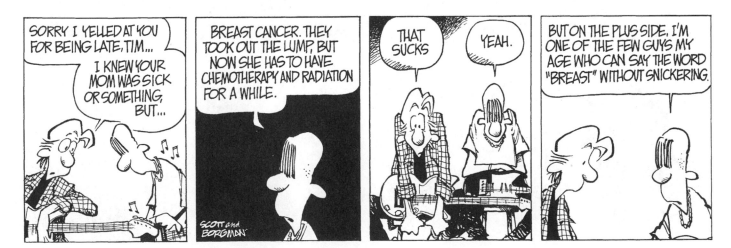

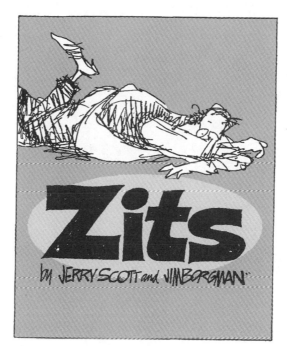

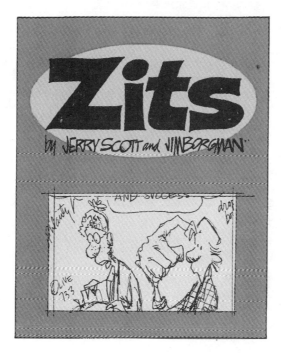

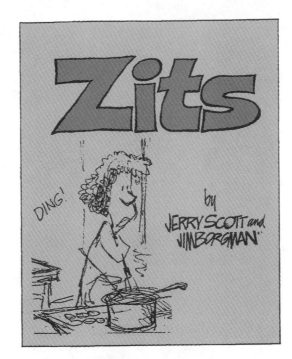

38

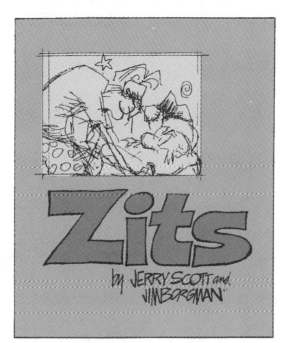

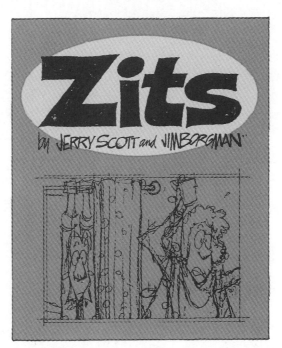

44

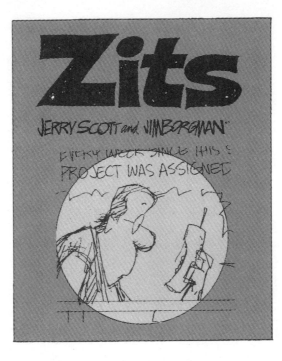

49

Panel 1: YOU GOT A DETENTION AT SCHOOL AND YOU DIDN'T TELL ME!
SO??

Panel 2: SCOTT and BORGMAN
THERE ARE A LOT OF THINGS IN MY LIFE I CHOOSE NOT TO TELL YOU ABOUT!

Panel 4: SUCH AS...?
STUPID! STUPID! STUPID! STUPID!

Panel 5: MY MOM WAS REALLY MAD THAT I DIDN'T TELL HER ABOUT GETTING THAT DETENTION.

Panel 6: AT FIRST SHE MADE ME PROMISE TO TELL HER EVERY SINGLE THING THAT HAPPENS AT SCHOOL
BUT I GOT HER TO CHANGE HER MIND ABOUT THAT.

Panel 7: HOW?
SCOTT and BORGMAN

Panel 8: BY TELLING HER EVERY SINGLE THING THAT HAPPENS AT SCHOOL.
OOH!

Panel 9: JEREMY, I WANT TO KNOW WHY YOU GOT A DETENTION AND I WANT TO KNOW NOW!
OKAY! OKAY!

Panel 10: HECTOR, AUTUMN and I WERE AT OUR LOCKERS WHEN THIS DELIVERY GUY WALKS UP and SAYS:
I'VE GOT THE 50,000 LIVE CRICKETS FOR MR. HEDGEWIG'S BIOLOGY LAB.
SCOTT and BORGMAN

Panel 11: NATURALLY WE WANTED TO BE AS HELPFUL AS POSSIBLE IN THE INTEREST OF SCIENCE...
NATURALLY

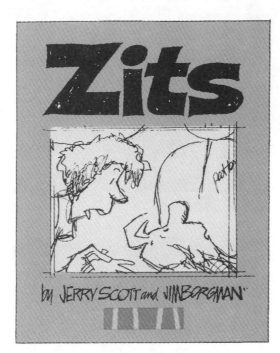

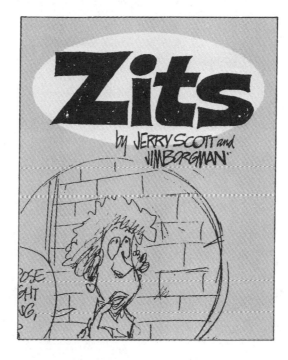

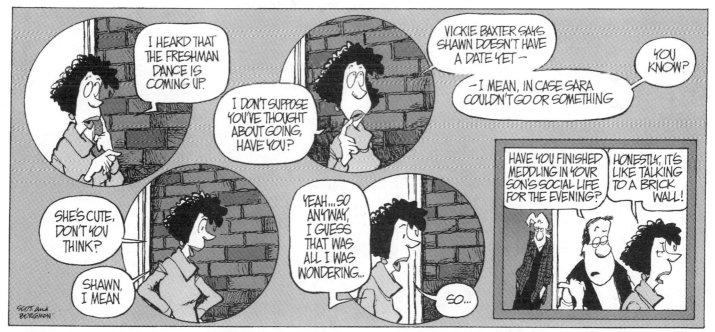

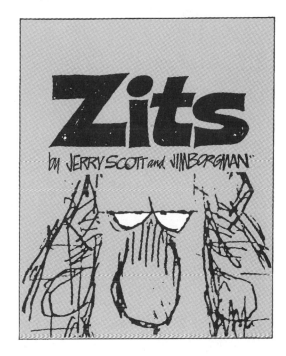

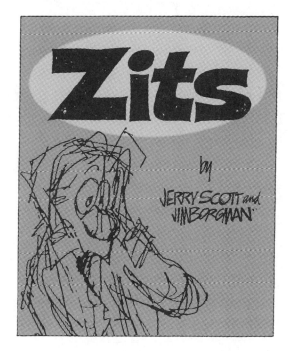

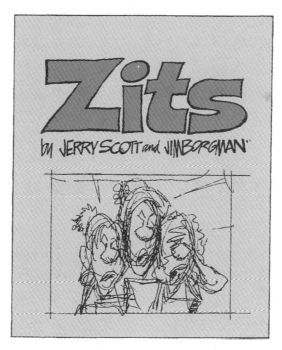

80

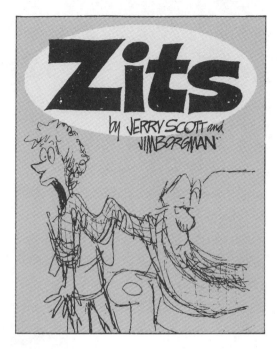

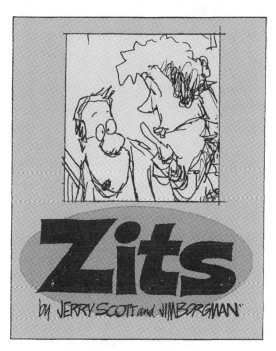

CRUNCH!

SKOOTCH! CRACK!
SNAP! CRUNCH! CRUNCH!

AHH.

JEREMY, HAVE YOU SEEN MY SUNGLASSES?

TECHNICALLY, NO.

HEY.

HEY.

YOU GOOD?

YEAH, I'M GOOD

YOU?

ABOUT THE SAME

GOOD

THAT WAS FAST

YEAH, WELL OUR HEART-TO-HEART TALKS DON'T LAST AS LONG AS THEY USED TO.

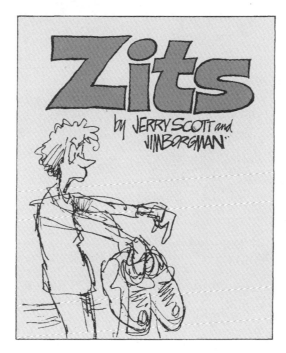

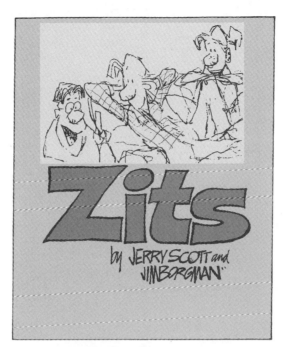

121

123

127

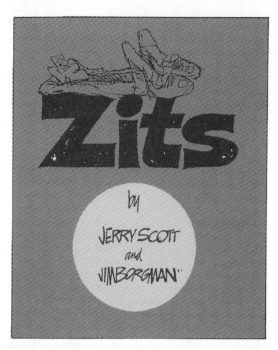